Under

Office Politics

in a week

PATRICK FORSYTH

Hodder & Stoughton

A MEMBER OF THE HODDER HEADLINE GROUP

Orders: please contact Bookpoint Ltd, 39 Milton Park, Abingdon, Oxon OX14 4TD. Telephone: (44) 01235 827720, Fax: (44) 01235 400454. Lines are open from 9.00 - 6.00, Monday to Saturday, with a 24 hour message answering service. Email address: orders@bookpoint.co.uk

British Library Cataloguing in Publication Data
A catalogue record for this title is available from The British Library

ISBN 0 340 757736

First published 1999

Impression number	10	9	8	7	6	5	4	3	2	1
Year	2005	2004	2003	2002	2001	2000	1999			

Typeset by Multiplex Techniques Ltd, St Mary Cray, Kent.
Printed in Great Britain for Hodder & Stoughton Educational, a division of Hodder Headline Plc, 338 Euston Road, London NW1 3BH by Cox & Wyman Ltd, Reading, Berkshire.

im the Institute of Management

FOUNDATION

The mission of the Institute of Management (IM) is to promote the art and science of management.

The Institute embraces all levels of management from student to chief executive and supports its own Foundation which provides a unique portfolio of services for all managers, enabling them to develop skills and achieve management excellence.

For information on the various levels and benefits of membership, please contact:

Department HS
Institute of Management
Cottingham Road
Corby
Northants NN17 1TT
Tel: 01536 204222
Fax: 01536 201651

This series is commissioned by the Institute of Management Foundation.

CONTENTS

INTRODUCTION

Office politics have predominantly negative connotations. The phrase itself summons up images of Machiavellian plotting and watching your back. If the office with no office politics exists it has not yet been discovered, so the only option for those working in an organisation is to recognise this fact and act accordingly.

Managers and executives are judged by results. To be successful, to achieve these results or hit the targets you are set, may well be a constant challenge, especially with increasingly competitive markets and unpredictable economic conditions. The phrase 'the only place where success comes before work is in the dictionary' is usually attributed to Vidal Sassoon, but whoever said it first it is likely to be true. Yet whatever work is necessary, and whatever skills must be cultivated to back up pure application, the challenge remains – and if circumstances and people conspire to make the task more difficult, this cannot be ignored. You have to react to the realities of office life.

Now, let us be clear. There is nothing wrong with healthy competition between people. Many would claim this is good, and certainly it is a simple fact of human nature. Nor is friction necessarily all bad. It can act as a catalyst to stimulate thought, creativity and ideas and make things happen that might otherwise not. While the worst aspects of office politics are certainly unconstructive, there are some ways in which it can work for you. But whatever the effects of office politics, they should never be regarded as 'just happening'. An active approach is necessary to minimise the negative effects that office politics may have on you, and to maximise any constructive ways in which it may help you.

This book examines how such constructive individual action should be approached. It is not a 'backstabbers' charter', rather it offers guidance to those wanting to increase their effectiveness and maximise any opportunities or methods available to assist this process, and ultimately to further their careers. In common with other books in this series, it divides its coverage into manageable topics, one for each day of the week:

Sunday	The realities of office life
Monday	Adopting the right approach
Tuesday	The power of personal image
Wednesday	The role of communication
Thursday	Management matters
Friday	Active responses and initiatives
Saturday	Consolidating your position

The realities of office life

Day One, and there is a need to start with a healthy dose of realism. Every organisation is a complex environment. And anyone working in one is subject to many different factors that either assist their success or make things more difficult. Success may be made more likely within an organisation that has, say, a constructive training policy, open communications or in which someone finds themselves working for an especially supportive boss. Alternatively, such things as a lack of clear objectives, pointless time-wasting bureaucracy, or persistently unclear instructions may hinder success. The range of factors is considerable and includes ones that are seemingly small or unimportant. For example, just not being invited to a particular meeting might be significant – either allowing you time to get on with something more important, or cutting you off from an opportunity to influence a decision.

But there is one factor that is perhaps more likely to exert an influence than any other, and that is people. Unless you are a freelancer or sole trader, working in an organisation automatically means you are interacting with others. Much of this interaction may be constructive. Other individuals may help and support what you do, team working may add a resource over and above individual skills, and ideas being discussed may lead to new thoughts, different action and greater success. But … and there is always a but:

People mean politics

People, however constructively they approach their jobs,

are not motivated solely by the desire to meet objectives and succeed in achieving the results they are charged with producing. They have their own agendas; some of which may help the general good, but others may not. Personal ambitions include:

- getting the job done
- increasing personal job satisfaction
- organising greater visibility
- impressing others
- securing greater rewards
- gaining greater authority
- taking on greater responsibilities
- beating others in a race for promotion
- obtaining additional perks.

The list above immediately shows the possibilities for office politics; for example the possibility of competition.

People seek outcomes to situations which fulfil their own personal ambitions. As people work hard to achieve what they want, it is a short step from simply pushing for it to pushing even harder – in a way that not only achieves what they want, but prevents or handicaps someone else in their intentions. Assertiveness becomes aggression, and brute force becomes the order of the day. Although this may be secretively devised, subtly or even invisibly deployed, brute force still describes it well – it has no purpose other than to achieve parochial personal advantage.

As we are being realistic today, it is worth considering other factors; for instance, some people are inherently less concerned about others than they might be. This may be because of their own feelings of inadequacy or incompetence (real or imagined), or alternatively some may have what is frankly best described as destructive streaks. These may be:

- wanting others to fail
- delighting in others' misfortunes
- seeing winning in terms of someone else losing
- using others
- liking the process of 'doing someone down' (irrespective of the effect on themselves)
- being a bully
- wanting the credit for everything
- letting their prejudices overrule practicality.

As always, the nature and scale of these destructive streaks may vary. Someone may simply be a bit ruthless in the way they set out to achieve some small step (like gaining the ubiquitous key to the Executive Washroom). Or, at worst, they may see an out-and-out backstabbing approach as their best route onto the Board, say, and be prepared to go to any lengths to succeed.

Appearances can be deceptive

Because of the way people approach their jobs, and many peoples' willingness to indulge, at least to some extent, in a political approach to what they do, it pays to remember that many of the signs around you in the organisation may be deceptive. Things are not always what they appear, and similarly, what people say can be deceptive, with hidden messages and agendas.

We all know the stock warning: always be wary of the person who starts by saying 'Trust me', 'Let me be honest' or 'I'm on your side'. This holds true as a warning to react by reading carefully between the lines as the communication continues. Aim to understand peoples'

motives, and do not necessarily think the best of them, or automatically give them the benefit of the doubt. Prudence is a good watchword in the political jungle of a typical organisation. Watch for and read the signs in:

- what is said
- how it is said
- announcements and decisions
- alliances and changes of alliance
- peoples' intentions and motivations
- the behaviour of others
- communications (from memos to meetings).

Forewarned is forearmed

So, one element of your judgement about everything needs to be to keep an eye on the political implications or possibilities. This might be best stated as watching for dangers and opportunities, because what you observe may provide an indication of either. People need to be regarded as potential friends or enemies; and sometimes they may be one on one occasion and another at a later time.

What you must do is link your own clear intention, purpose and objectives to a way of working that reflects the environment – that is the political environment. You cannot work in isolation, in the sense of pursuing your intentions as if others cannot affect your progress towards them. They will definitely affect the pursuit of your own goal. The only question is whether others can assist your progress, or alternatively, whether you need to ensure that others do not prevent it being made less likely. In either case, you need to consider what action might be necessary on your part to accentuate the positive, rather than negative, effects of other people.

This sort of thinking needs to instill itself in every aspect of your judgement. For example, who – exactly – do you take into your confidence, and how much and how soon? When should you ask advice? How much should you publicise your success (or hide anything that is less than successful)? Who should you know and who should know you? And what do you want other people to think of you? All these kinds of questions are important. All demand you make considered judgements about the way you approach office life.

Adopting an appropriate approach

The out-and-out obvious politician may be adopting an approach that actually does them more harm than good. Most organisations contain some individuals who are well known for their ruthless opportunism and politicking. People may sensibly avoid them, or at least avoid crossing swords with them. Their ploys are anticipated and ultimately that gets them nowhere.

You have to decide just how to play things. Adopt the brash approach illustrated above and you may gain nothing. Avoid or ignore all the intrigue and you may be left on the sidelines and others will get the better of you. Just what is the best way forward? First consider some of the approaches people may adopt.

These include:

- *The publicist* who approaches everything with an eye on how people will see them. They want the credit for everything, and always want to be the centre of attention. They may take this to extraordinary limits, spending long hours and considerable effort ensuring no tiny opportunity is overlooked.
- *The mole* who has a surreptitious approach, hiding out of sight. Operating secretively behind closed doors, they are nevertheless dodging the system and working hard to get just what they want out of everything that goes on.
- *The empire builder* whose whole approach is to expand their field of influence. They seek for themselves a presence in, if not responsibility for, everything.

There are doubtless more types that could be characterised in this way – including some that are much more aggressive than those listed. Remember, such approaches are not mutually exclusive; elements of all of these may be included by some in their overall approach. Seniority also has a bearing. It is easier to empire build if you have the power to do so, for example.

The specific approach you adopt will depend to some extent on the style of those around you, and the culture of the organisation you work in. Openness, for example, could be an advantage in a normally secretive environment, but might upset someone who was unable to envisage anything other than a secretive approach.

Certainly your approach needs to consider others. This does not mean only the prime players. It includes others who, while themselves more neutral in the overall gameplan, are potentially a source of help in specific ways.

People power

While many, even most, people are actual or potential adversaries, or at least competitors, many are also allies. The latter may help actively or just in the background, and you can never have too many people like this. Some will be an inherent part of your life, but others need to be found and cultivated and you should never underestimate how much systematic and sustained effort that takes. Consider people who:

- are sources of information
- arrange or allow introductions to others
- assist your cause, directly, for whatever reason
- boost your morale or enthusiasm.

Such people include those within but also outside your immediate organisation. Outside contacts can include past colleagues, suppliers, social contacts, and more. Everybody, from people you meet at a conference to those you sit on a committee with, is a potential ally.

This is an area that cannot be left to chance. You may feel that you are essentially well connected, but contacts always need expanding. Those who move out of your network need replacing and changed circumstances demand new allies. The networking process is fundamental to holding your own in the political arena and you need to actively consider *who* should be 'on your list', and how you *manage the process* to keep contacts fresh and useful.

Who should you select?

There are a variety of categories; indeed the first step of thinking this through should be to systematically consider the categories, before you think of individual people. In other words the starting point is asking who you *should* know, rather than just who you do know.

Categories of contact

- *Sources of information*: those who know things, know how to find out things, are prepared to share things with you and, in some cases, delight in being known as information givers.
- *Gatekeepers*: those who are less important in their own right but more for their ability to allow (or deny) access to others.
- *Opportunity spotters*: including those who are in a position to provide opportunities that help your job performance.

- *Influencers*: those who are able and willing to make things happen for you, and have the clout or seniority to do so.
- *Mentors*: those who elect to provide you with on-going advice, support and encouragement.
- *Developers*: those from whom you actively learn (it is good if your immediate boss is one, and others may be needed too).
- *Stimulators*: those whose company or comment acts as a catalyst and spurs on your creativity.
- *Role models*: those whose example you can learn from (either with or without contact and advice from them).
- *Soul mates*: those who you mix with socially or semi-socially and whose friendship helps keep you sane and on track.
- *Swappers*: those with skills complementary to your own (who, for example, help you edit a report in return for your help in rehearsing a presentation).
- *Rising stars*: those less senior than yourself, who can nevertheless help, in part with their fresh ideas (and who may want you to regard them as a protégé and help them too).
- *Your staff*: while you may not want to embroil all of them in the detail of your schemes, they should essentially be a positive resource.
- *Devil's advocates*: those prepared to critique your plans, thinking or ideas in a constructive way that stimulates a final conclusion.

You may need to tie in with people in all these categories. The list is not definitive, nor are the categories mutually exclusive – one person may fulfill a number of roles for you. Hierarchies are usually unimportant to this kind of contact, and those you liaise with may include people from all levels and parts of the organisation. Trust is important however, and no contact will thrive if either party feels unsure of the relationship. Furthermore, as has already been said, being well connected does not just happen – any list of contacts needs work.

How do you manage your contacts?

The first task is to assemble a useful network. This must be done progressively and in all sorts of ways. Some contacts are known to you and just need developing. Others need establishing or seeking out, a process that can occur by spotting opportunities (e.g. talking to someone you sit next to at a conference), or which must be more prescribed (e.g. resolving to get to know someone in Finance and doing so).

Beyond that the process will only work if you:

- *spend time maintaining contact* – it is all to easy to find you have not spoken to someone for six months and rapport is starting to decline
- *see the process as two-way* – people are more inclined to help those who help them
- *keep promises* – be a reliable contact
- *return favours* – for example by swapping tasks
- *make the process acceptable* – the pleasantries and courtesies are important and it should be interesting and fun
- *keep good records* – not just of names and addresses, but a record of contacts to maintain continuity.

A network of people is the foundation resource of your political strategy. Having the right network cannot be left to chance. You need to have clear intentions, make and maintain the necessary contacts, use them systematically and keep some records to help foster the whole process. If this makes it seem somewhat scheming, then so be it. It is a necessary and important part of organisational life. People, and one's individual contacts and interactions, are what makes working in an organisation possible, interesting and enjoyable. So there is a wide range of rewards stemming from taking an active approach.

A basis for action

There is an old saying that it is not what you know that is important, but who you know. In fact both are important in the office arena. Information is power, as they say, and you need to know what is going on. Who you know is also important for keeping up to date. But the who is important in a broader sense. You need allies. And you need to recognise and avoid enemies. Do not assume that everyone who is apparently neutral is on your side, and remember that some people who intentionally put out clear 'Friend' signals are not really friends; and vice versa. Certain types probably need active avoidance, or at least constant wariness. For instance, those who are:

- untrustworthy or unpredictable
- difficult, more likely to raise your stress levels than your hopes
- cynical, dismissing something as impossible, only because they would find it so

- obviously in competition, who do need watching
- in strong alliances with others who you want to avoid, for whatever reason
- unable to keep secrets.

Tread carefully; think about how you are perceived by those around you in the organisation. Adopt an approach that is likely to help you get the job done (results always matter), and that is also likely to position you to advantage in the longer term.

The following chapters will help you decide how to adopt strategies to assist you to survive and prosper in the corporate jungle. You have already taken the first step if you accept that such strategies are necessary, and plan and act accordingly.

Adopting the right approach

Every business needs goals. As it is with a business, so too with a career. You need to look ahead; even far ahead. If you make no attempt to control your destiny, you may find that events will manipulate you – and so will other people. This can be avoided by effective planning ahead.

You are a major influence on your own career success. Office politics can be described as an environmental influence which either inherently helps or hinders your progress, or alternatively can be made to assist it, rather in the way that market dynamics and competition influence an organisation's commercial success. What happens is what happens, but the final impact of those circumstances will be changed to include your reaction to the situation. However, you can only manage the politics that surround you to your advantage if you are clear what you are trying to achieve. Instant, maybe even defensive, action will do more harm than good – if you do not have clear aims in mind.

The personal planning process is essentially similar to business planning, and revolves around four key questions:

1. Where am I now? (situation analysis)
2. Where do I want to get? (objective setting)
3. How will I get there? (strategy formulation)
4. How will I know when I get there? (control)

Each is worth an individual comment.

Where am I now?

This question deserves more than an answer of a few words or just your job title. Some analysis of your current situation, where you are starting from, is a sound basis for moving forward. This is a rolling process, initial thinking – which can range from 'back of an envelope' notes to more formal analysis – should be updated and revised over time.

Ask yourself:

- What have I achieved in the past (and how has this come about)?
- How many of my needs does my current job fulfill?
- What have I done, acquired or learnt in the past that might stand me in good stead for the future?
- Who have I worked with in the past and what connections do they have or how otherwise might they assist my progress?

A comprehensive review is worthwhile; you could well be surprised by how much you have achieved and how much that can help you in taking the next steps forwards.

Where do I want to get?

Here analysis must include two factors: ambition, which is what you want, and realism, which is what is possible. Consider:

Your preferences
This is a good starting point and you must always be clear about your likes and dislikes. Ask yourself what kind of work you want to do. What characteristics should it involve (e.g. allowing your creativity free reign), what

should it ideally include (e.g. international travel), and what rewards should it bring (financial and otherwise)? Do not forget the satisfactions involved, it is no good fighting your way to the top if your day to day existence is then a nightmare.

The environment

Here you need to add a note of realism. If the field in which you work only operates in the UK, then it is unlikely to satisfy any desire you might have for international travel (unless you are able to influence it in that direction). Consider how the size, nature and philosophy of the business domain in which you are involved and also, importantly, the people around you, are all likely to influence your intentions. Look further afield, asking how elements such as society, the environment or market change may affect matters. For example, new technology might arrive and change the whole basis on which an industry operates.

The resources

Here, see what exists, principally within your own organisation, that might act as a resource. Is the organisation cash rich or penny pinching? What skills does it utilise? What strengths does it have? Does it have physical assets that make it attractive to work for? (For example, do you see progress as moving from regional to national matters and relocating to Head Office?)

Your competencies
Be honest here. Consider what you are good at, what you might become good at and what is never going to be your forte. You will do best by playing to your strengths (getting even better at the things you are good at), but also by expanding your strengths (increasing the range of things you are good at).

Objectives
Then, with all this in mind, you can set objectives. These are most useful if they are specific. It is little good just saying to yourself – *I want to be rich*. But how rich? How soon? Spell out some intentions that are measurable, that relate to your analysis (so that they are realistic, play to your strengths and make sense in terms of the area in which you work) and put a timetable on them. By all means aim high: it is easier to settle for a little less than what you would really like than it is to gear up your plans again to aim higher when you have wasted too much time aiming elsewhere.

How will I get there?

Objectives are the planned results of your actions; the strategy is the route you use to get there. For example, you may aim for a seat on the Board, but come to see the best way of achieving this as excelling in some specific functional area first. The two intentions build on each other,

the first is a means to an end and getting where you want to go in one big jump may be too much to hope for.

Your strategy or plan of action need not be complete, indeed, unless you had second sight, how could it be? Corporate life is just too unpredictable. But you should have a clear idea of the main actions you plan to take and the broad path you will follow. *Tactics* are the means by which – day by day – you turn your thinking and your broad intentions into action that makes sense, and by which you respond to the detailed events that surround you.

In forming a strategy – some way ahead – you could do worse than copy the technique of SWOTs analysis. SWOTs stands for: Strengths, Weaknesses, Opportunities and Threats and is most often used to analyse the internal (S and W) and external (O and T) factors on which a company's future plans must be predicated. But these are exactly the right headings to have in mind yourself, and a strategy must certainly accommodate all four factors. For instance, not allowing for a weakness, such as not being able to give effective presentations, would lessen your chances of success.

How will I know when I get there?

The key here is to *control* the process. You may well recognise it when you achieve an ultimate goal, however you should be clear about how far you have got at any particular point along the way. This is a prerequisite to fine-tuning what you are doing, adjusting the plan to take advantage of, or avoid, new or changed factors as you go along. In reality, prediction is usually difficult. Success has at least as much to do with adapting as you go along as with simply anticipating the inevitable, as it were, and then giving yourself the credit for it.

A strong foundation

All this thinking provides a firm foundation for how you proceed. But the ebb and flow of office politics may create impacts that:

- assist you
- hinder you
- are neutral
- provide opportunities for advancement
- forewarn you of pitfalls.

In other words, some external things inevitably affect your situation – but so do you. Probably the most significant effects are where you actively influence matters, spotting a likely hazard and stepping aside, or taking advantage of things as they progress. Rarely can we spot an uninterrupted chain of opportunity, but sometimes this is the case and the long term must certainly always be born in mind alongside the short term. Indeed, it is possible to jump at some dramatic short-term advantage and only later to find that long-term factors negate that advantage. This is especially true where people are concerned, as they should be thought of as long-term resources, rather than used for short-term gain. This is the essence of the old saying about being nice to people on the way up, otherwise you may rue it as you cross paths with them on the way down again.

What is required is an active approach, well directed and focused, and tuned to take advantage of opportunities – or sidestep setbacks – as time goes by.

The power of personal image

Whatever the complexities of the politics of organisations, one thing is certain – appearances count. Forget 'never judge a book by its cover', because people do. How people perceive you inevitably colours their image of you. They make judgements about what sort of person you are, where you sit in the office hierarchy (official and unofficial), whether you are to be regarded as friend or foe, and what power they perceive you have to promote or protect yourself. Consider exactly how other people see you, and you will avoid stereotypical labelling such as the computer geek, the grey accountant, the absent-minded boffin or the office Romeo.

Remember that judgements are made, even snap decisions, and incorporate this in your personal approach to appearance. You should:

- accept the importance of appearance
- be conscious of both the positive and negative sides
- actively respond to the ways in which people see you.

The starting point to action here involves some self-analysis. If you know how you want people to see you, then you can actively seek to achieve the effect you want. This may seem easy. You may want to look powerful, persuasive or professional. But many such fine sounding words are in fact just umbrella terms – you must ask what qualities does being professional, say, really involve? Being professional means being:

- expert
- well organised
- well prepared
- confident
- knowledgeable
- experienced
- trustworthy
- honest
- approachable
- good at listening
- powerful
- diplomatic
- good at communicating
- loyal.

All of these qualities encompass a range of possibilities – witness the many ways in which you might be well organised. The list is not definitive, though some of the qualities listed are certainly important for most people (and we will return to communication soon, giving it a section on its own). You can probably add more, including some factors that are more specific to your own particular job. Maybe you need to come over as financially aware, as a good negotiator or a whiz with information technology. Maybe it is important that you are professional in a less conventional sense: seen to be powerful because you have the ear of someone specific on the Board, say.

In any case, several points are clear. First, however you look at it, such a list contains a number of factors: perhaps a considerable number. Second, for the most part the factors represent possibilities, that is you can *choose* to project a feeling of, say, being approachable even if this is not your natural inclination. Most people actively boost the way they are seen in some respects. You may reckon you are well organised, for instance, but still want to give an impression of supreme organisational skill on one particular occasion, or perhaps to one particular person.

These two points should work together. You should have clear objectives for how you want to appear, as well as working at really being it. This may mean recognising weaknesses. If you are naturally bad at self-organisation, then you may need to actually get organised, and develop this as a revised part of the way you operate, rather than just seek to *appear* well organised. In other words, the number of factors included is complex and needs to be considered in conjunction with how you are and how you want to be, as well as how you wish to be seen. The overall impression must not become too contrived, especially not obviously so, which would quickly be self-defeating. For the most part all that is necessary is some slight exaggeration of characteristics to ensure they are visible where required.

Looking the part

An obvious starting point with regard to personal image is your dress and other elements of your literal appearance.

It should be said at once that the objective here is not to stereotype you or remove anything of character and replace it by a universally bland image. The days of the organisation where every businessman, for example, was expected to wear the same (plain white shirt, grey suit, black shoes and conservative tie) are largely gone, and dress now involves a much wider range of acceptable options. Women too, appearing on the corporate scene in larger numbers and more senior positions than in the past, have wide choice. However, you do need to consider what is suitable. Indeed, you need to consider what 'suitable' means.

Some things are obviously sensible – universally. I will use a man as my example. Clean shoes, a well pressed suit and a smart tie may always be acceptable; but there are exceptions. If a jacket and slacks is the norm in your office, then wearing that will be fine and a suit may even be too heavy. Be sensible about making individual judgements. If you work in an advertising agency or some other creative company, then a suit, particularly a conventional business suit, might be regarded as wildly overdressed. Conversely, there may be a good deal to be gained by being the only one in a more conservative group who dares to wear a bright suit or a really jazzy tie, so this could be the right decision – for some people. The most important thing is to think about it. If you simply emerge bleary-eyed from bed and reach for whatever looks reasonably clean, you may miss some tricks.

Beyond sensible consideration and judgement lie two further approaches. They both involve more formal consideration.

Power dressing

Power dressing as a phrase and a concept comes, of course, from the United States. The thinking is that everything about you needs to shout confidence and that money should be no object in achieving what you want. So, you buy the best suits (tailor-made), you wear the best watch, carry the finest leather briefcase and adorn your desk with silver photograph frames or whatever other trinkets you believe will enhance your image. The dangers, especially outside of the United States, are obvious. There is a scale involved in the way such things should be regarded. At one end the approach is so low key or inappropriate that you are either invisible or marked down. And at the other, you are seriously over the top or seen as being ridiculously pretentious.

So, somewhere between having your briefcase tied together with string and dressing as if you are a lottery winner who should not be working at all, is what is right for you. Think about it.

Professional advice
Alternatively, get someone else to think about it for you, because the second more formal approach is to use one of a number of image consultants to advise you on how you should dress and look. This is a substantial step towards spin doctoring, and you may be able to think of politicians whose image is professionally 'managed' yet who you do not regard as any sort of advertisement for such a method. However, some people do use such help and are well pleased by it. If appearance is very important to you, and if you can afford it, this could be worth a try.

Paraphernalia

What you have around you also speaks volumes about you (so maybe this book should be sold with an optional brown paper cover in case the wrong people see you reading it!). More seriously, there are many things that you have about you that contribute to your overall image. Certainly your office or workstation, is one major one. It acts as a kind of billboard to those seeking to form judgements about you. Signals are given off by an office, according to:

- its location
- its size
- its purpose (does it include a meeting table/chairs?)
- its organisation
- its busyness
- its contents
- its embellishments.

The situation is similar with regard to yourself and your more personal accoutrements. Here again there is no right approach or single solution for dealing with any particular area. The following list is designed to get you thinking about different implications and perhaps prompt you to think of those factors that you can adjust or arrange yourself to help create the positive image you want.

A question of impact

- The best computer on your desk may be good, but can you work it?
- Are six e-mail addresses making you look more important or pretentious?
- Is a fat Filofax best or a slim one?
- Does your electronic organiser really save you time, or does being seen to wipe out all of your telephone number list make you look less than efficient?

- Should certificates (such as membership of the Institute of Management) be on show?
- Is a row of cheap pens in your outside jacket pocket a good idea?

You could turn such a list into a veritable audit of questions regarding many different issues and your current practice. One such is worth individual comment:

Image on the move

Stand 100 metres from the Accountant's office (or whoever else may be concerned) and whisper 'Company car', and you may hear a grown-up whimper like a child. Few things cause such aggravation or divisiveness. No one, but no one, seems satisfied with their company car. It is too small, too big, too ordinary, too old or produces too great a tax bill. Cars are not just a means of getting from A to B, they are part of their owner's persona.

This means that cars, too, represent an element of the image you wish to present to others. A Rolls Royce for everybody is not advocated, but influencing the policy to try to get something you are happy with is a good idea. You have to balance different factors. A smart coupe may look impressive parked outside the office, but if you regularly have to get the bulky luggage associated with, say, two small children in, it may not be the right choice. In any case, in some organisations you may be better regarded by showing restraint than by going conspicuously over the top. As one example of really working the system, I remember hearing of one man, moved to his organisation's Singapore office, who had a company motorbike. Cars are expensive there. Taxis are cheap, and the island is only a few miles across. The motorbike was fun, made an impression, gave him mobility if he wanted and the arrangement saved a considerable sum of money, some of which he negotiated into a higher salary. Remember too the external image: a customer may interpret too good a car as a sign of excessive prices.

Other travel factors can also influence your image, for example:

- travelling first or second class on trains
- flying economy or business class
- taking the tunnel from London to Paris to save time
- the kind of hire car you use.

Whenever you travel, or arrange to travel, someone will be taking note of how you do it. Like so much else, a sense of political awareness is necessary as you make decisions in this area.

On top of things

A final area of consideration links to everything already said in this section. Most, if not all, jobs demand that you perform well. Results must be achieved and targets hit, and you are more likely to be regarded with respect, as a power to be reckoned with, if you are seen as an effective performer. Of course, there are those who keep their heads down and who are not actually all that effective, yet who seem to succeed in a certain amount of manipulation. This is difficult to sustain long term, however, and in most likely future scenarios, increased pressure to achieve results and uncertain and difficult markets and economic conditions will make the success of this strategy even less certain.

Whatever your job, achieving the results you want will demand a range of knowledge and skills. Remaining well equipped and competent in a changing world is clearly only sensible. However, some prerequisites of success are specifically visible and thus worth a mention here. It is surely true, for example, that you are more likely to deliver appropriate results if you are well organised; therefore, you are more likely to be taken seriously if you are *seen to be* well organised. Consider some examples of practice that gives a positive impression:

- *Punctuality*: turning up for things on time and hitting deadlines takes some effort, but is worthwhile in terms of the impression of efficiency it creates.
- *Time management*: managing your time, your projects and diary and creating strong productivity is also well worthwhile. Good time management can increase productivity significantly. So, although there is no magic formula and the secret lies in the details and creating the right disciplines, becoming good in this way is really a necessity.
- *Tidiness*: literally *looking* well organised. Your office, your desk, your paperwork all can assist you in putting over the image that you have decided upon.

Rather like a medieval army lining up on the hill overlooking the likely battlefield, you must decide the position from which you operate. A position of being regarded as effective, well organised, confident and on top of things makes sense. Whether you want to work quietly and unobtrusively in the background, or lead from the front, how you come across to other people is important. This needs consideration and it is not a matter that can be left to chance.

Summary

Appearance – in all its manifestations – should not be dismissed as cosmetic irrelevance. It is an area well worth some thought. There are few rules as to how to proceed, other than that you need to work at it and implement a series of considered judgements to get the balance right. If people are going to see you as influential, as a power to be reckoned with in whatever way and to whatever degree you want, then the sum total of the many ways in which others perceive you must be actively designed to work for you. The objective is to directly influence how people relate to you. Simplistically, this means that if you look like a doormat, you tend to get trodden on, and if you appear to have clout, the respect you command increases. When considering how to create the right impression, remember:

- you only get one chance to make a first impression, so it had better be good
- the details matter and contribute to the total effect (for good or bad)
- perception *is* reality, people really will judge you on appearances
- consistency of overall approach helps to build an image cumulatively
- 'it pays to advertise'.

In an organisational environment another factor is closely linked with appearance. Communication in all its forms is ubiquitous in the office, and there is more to it than just transferring information – every time you communicate, *how* you do it says something about you. We will look at this in Wednesday's section.

The role of communication

If office politics is concerned with human interaction, then communication – without which there would be no such interaction – is vital. What you communicate and how you do so is the lifeblood of your political standing; and this applies to both formal and informal communications. You may rue or bless the day you submitted a particular report, or even the few words you exchanged with someone in passing in the corridor.

Consider the nature of communicating for a moment. Communication goes on amongst people all the time. Much of it demands little thought, and understanding is successfully achieved. Some communication struggles slightly – 'what do you mean exactly?' – but succeeds despite its imperfections. But, in fact, communication is inherently difficult and most people can all too easily conjure up memories of past communication breakdowns that confirm this. The cause may be simple. 'No price too high' does not mean the same as 'No. Price too high', and the fax in which the full stop is omitted may not just cause confusion, it may lead to bankruptcy. On the other hand, the officespeak and gobbledegook which passes for communication in some organisations may bury every message in an impenetrable fog.

So, accurate communication is a sound basis for success, whether this just means getting your message across or creating a specific profile for yourself that matches your personal aims and intentions. This means it is worthwhile to:

- recognise that communication can be difficult
- think before communicating
- deliver, consciously, exactly the message you want
- add the emphasis and feeling you want.

It also means that you should be very careful in interpreting the communications that are directed at you.

Reading between the lines

As everyone has their own point of view and their own agenda, communications often have more than one layer. You need to watch out for phrases with a subtext, such as: 'This is a great opportunity for you (and one I can well do without)', or 'It's no trouble at all (I will be calling in the debt soon)'. Some of these are ubiquitous – nobody means 'Have you got a couple of minutes?' literally, and practically everyone seems to use the computer as an excuse: 'Sorry, the computer's down' (I haven't input the data yet). What is more, many communications are unclear because part of the message is hidden to some extent. For example, imagine someone says 'If you think it's a good idea, I suggest you go ahead'. If it works out they will say they supported the idea (and perhaps want some of the credit), if it is a disaster then they never said *they* thought it was right. Some element of double meaning is perhaps necessary, but it is worth forming a view on just how many such overtones you need to look for in communications received from your colleagues and contacts, interpreting them accordingly.

While messages from some people can be taken at face value, it may help to grade those you deal with to some extent, as below:

- *The devious*: who always seem to inject a hidden meaning.
- *The very devious*: whose communications have more layers than an onion.
- *The downright Machiavellian*: whose subtext is actively disruptive.

Take messages on board with an appropriate degree of circumspection. Bear in mind that it is often those messages that appear most innocuous which should be interpreted with the most care, perhaps particularly those that make strident attempts to appear without guile. Warning phrases include such introductory remarks as: 'Trust me' or 'Let me be honest' – and added sincerity that does not ring true 'I only say this to help…'.

All this works both ways of course; people will try to read between the lines of messages you give them and you need to be clear about just what you are trying to say.

A variety of elements need watching for (or using). These include:

- *Exaggeration*: too much removes all credibility, too little and your message may lack power.
- *Flattery*: a little, appropriately used, really does go a long way; you might spot it at a hundred paces but that does not mean others do not respond positively (and if you found yourself agreeing with this thought, you have just been flattered – so it can work!).
- *Generalities or vagueness*: this may just be a sign of imprecise communication, but it could be an attempt to mislead (for example, when exactly will something be done if someone says 'leave it with me I will see to it at once'?).

- *Introspection*: too much that starts 'I think…' may be off-putting and could sell itself short, especially if it is actually the result of considerable research or can be backed up by significant proof.
- *Big words*: and similarly phrases, are a classic hiding place for precise meaning (saying that something can only go ahead after 'initiating project recording status' might be off-putting, and only mean a copy of the instruction needs to be put on file in Central Administration).
- *Jargon*: unless pitched right, can act as a smokescreen between people with similar levels of understanding.

Similarly, *precision and description* add to the likelihood of communication achieving its purpose. So, think what you mean to say or write, say what you mean and double check that the right message has got across. And never act on messages coming to you if you are not exactly clear what they mean. It may only take a moment to check, and without that you may find you have allowed yourself to be manipulated.

Without words

A major amount of the information transferred is non-verbal. Some of this is obvious: the sanctimonious smile that says 'I told you so', or the raised hand that says 'No interruptions' may be unmistakable. Some study, and thus knowledge, of body language (an inexact science, but useful to a degree) may help on occasion. There are certainly physical areas where there are signs to be sent or received, and care is necessary with regard to:

- *Space*: in the sense of proximity is very important. People want appropriate personal space, and someone getting in their 'intimate zone' may make them very uneasy. Suitable distancing prevents discomfort, whereas too little space creates pressure and distraction.
- *Touch*: physical contact is also something to be handled (sic) with care. A hand on an arm may be interpreted as a friendly gesture – or as grounds for sexual harassment. A 'wet' handshake is a universal sign of lack of clout, but crushing someone to the pain threshold is not going to impress either.
- *Eye contact*: like so much else a balance needs to be found. Those who never meet anyone's eye are always seen as devious, those who never let go of eye contact can appear to be putting the other person under undue pressure.
- *Position and posture*: this is the heartland of body language. Folded arms can signal a negative response. Leaning forward can express interest or enthusiasm. A fist banged on the table certainly gives a point greater force, but might be taken as a sign of loss of control.
- *Expression*: a smile may lighten a difficult moment, or be taken as inappropriate flippancy.

The moral here is to adopt a heightened consciousness about such things, to deploy them with care and read between the lines not only in terms of words, but of physical signs too.

There are other non-verbal manifestations of office politics at work, which are not physical in the sense of body language, but physical as opposed to theoretical. Very real physical difficulties are sometimes created to intentionally

put someone off balance. If you are asked to attend a meeting at 7-30am, make a presentation in a tiny room that will not allow the use of the overhead projector needed to show your slides, or given an impossible deadline – then there is always a chance that someone is trying to make you fail. Forewarned is forearmed, however. Getting over such a hurdle, taking it in your stride, and not letting it dilute the effectiveness of something and the fact may well show – and score you points with other members of a group.

Again the moral here is vigilance and care.

People difficulties

The problems of communication touched on so far can normally be surmounted with a bit of thought. Or they would be if people were not so contrary. Misjudge them and you compound any problem. Now people come in all shapes and sizes as it were, indeed it would be a dull old world if we were all the same. But certain people take exaggerated positions and adopt styles designed, sometimes in an ill-advised way, to augment their own powerbase.

You must expect to cross paths with, at a minimum, the following:

- *The 'row at all costs' type*: who feel there is always a corner to fight and that taking a heavy line is always best. Any incident is exaggerated, grudges are easily felt and an end is never heard of anything contentious. Joining battle may simply compound the difficulty and prolong the problem, as their stance is not based on rational argument. Concentrate on future matters and bypass the problem.
- *The 'rude by nature' type*: who are not prompted by specific incidents, they are just plain rude. There is even less to be gained by joining battle here, keep your cool, keep smiling and refuse to rise to the bait (something that will only encourage further attacks). Keep conversations factual and take some satisfaction from knowing that they know you are refusing to let them get to you.
- *The 'just a minute' type*: timewasters with apparently nothing much to do who seem intent on knocking your productivity for six by turning every simple exchange into a full-scale performance. Insist on getting down to business or you will never achieve anything with them; if you can do this while still persuading them that you are a good listener, you will have an ally for life.

- *The 'know it all' type*: who are forever airing their superiority and hate having their views challenged. They are also potential allies if dealt with appropriately. Only challenge when you are sure of your facts and recognise that doing this while acknowledging their expertise can be diplomatically worthwhile.
- *The 'tongue-tied' type*: from whom you cannot get anything by way of information. If they are in possession of information that can help you, then cultivating good questioning techniques is useful (do not ask – 'do you know anything about this?' because it is a closed question, and too easily prompts a negative answer or simple 'No'; rather say 'tell me what you know about this'.
- *The 'double-checker' type*: who are suspicious of everything and want proof of everything. Argument may create an enemy; do not rush things and trust can be built up.

You can doubtless think of further categories. Note also that each category comes in various forms. For example, a senior person needs different handling from someone at a more junior or less influential level. And, as ever, not everything is always as it seems. Someone may be unwilling to give information because they are nervous or tongue-tied; or because they want to keep something from you and want you to perceive them as nervous or tongue-tied in order to achieve that.

Whoever you engage in communication, it is a process that demands care. There is considerable satisfaction in judging things just right. For example, if a display of real firmness seems to be called for, works and makes all future exchanges easier and clearer, then you see the advantage of an approach that involves thinking it through. Conversely, an ill-considered outburst can mark you down as irrational, difficult and to be kept at arms' length, just when you need somebody's active and willing support.

Coping with conflict

There are, unfortunately, occasions when communication becomes outright conflict. You then have to decide what line to take in response. There are a number of possible options including the following approaches:

- *All-out attack*: here you decide to fight, knowing that one party must lose – them. This makes it necessary to categorise them as wrong and yourself as right. Even if you win, it may sacrifice any sort of working relationship with the person for the future.
- *Withdrawal*: this avoids the immediate problem, but leaves the real issue unchanged and no greater understanding between parties.
- *Capitulation*: you can give in. This may seem an option sometimes (either for a quiet life or to preserve good relations), but can lead to dissatisfaction and create problems for the future if you become seen as a doormat.
- *Compromise*: meeting people half way (or somewhere in between that is acceptable to both) is another way forward.
- *Creating change*: here conflict is viewed as normal but constructive – we look for debate and aim to find a way forward that is satisfactory to both parties.

The development of good people-handling skills is usually a prerequisite for the successful office politician. Without them, instinctive 'get off my back' or other defensive or aggressive postures, may damage your standing.

The right method of communication

An important aspect of communication is the method. Telephone someone and get bogged down because your argument is ill thought out and you may achieve nothing – or only succeed in alienating them. Write a well judged letter to meet the same objective and you may have instant agreement.

Methods differ. Telephone is voice only, no body language to augment the message and description may be difficult. Confident presentations can bolster a weak case and make a strong one irresistible. People can find written communication, which is useful to get down a full case without interruption, the most difficult. It is seen as a chore, dashed off in a formalised 'officespeak' style, yet provides permanent reference and any ill-judged phrases – there in black and white – may return to haunt you.

Always:

- review the possible communications methods
- assess their potential advantages and disadvantages
- focus on the likely results
- choose whatever seems most likely to achieve your purpose.

Sometimes the right decision involves multiple methods (something is put over at a departmental meeting, and then confirmed and recorded in writing). Sometimes an unexpected method adds weight (praise of someone at a meeting is much more powerful than a private word). Always it is more important to consider the effect of things than the ease of things. It may seem easy to make a quick telephone call, however consideration may well show that a written record of something is important, even if acting to produce one will take longer.

On the page

Let us investigate written communication by way of an example of a particular method. Every time you put pen to paper (or more commonly these days, fingers to keyboard) what you write not only puts over a message, it says something about you. The kind of person you are, the weight you have within the organisation, the likelihood of others regarding you as friend or foe – all spill out between the lines.

So, adopt an inappropriately over formal (or over informal) style, deploy a welter of impenetrable jargon, take ten pages to say what others feel could be encapsulated in a couple of sentences or come over as smug, self-righteous or condescending – and you will create effects that are the opposite of what you want.

A moment considering the ubiquitous memo quickly shows how wrong or mixed motivations can create paperwork that does nothing to enhance an image of power and competence, but actively gets the writer regarded as lightweight. We have all received examples of the following types of memo:

- *The 'display of power' memo*: which exists in writing, or goes on at length, only to make a point about the writer's authority. It says 'do this', or sometimes 'it is only a suggestion but do bear in mind who's making it'.
- *The 'rambling' memo*: which makes many points, in a random 'and another thing' fashion, all of which act as camouflage hiding the real core message or making it difficult to understand. This may be due to sloppy writing and is even worse in longer documents such as a report.
- *The 'for a rainy day' memo*: most often containing no information of immediate value, but sent so that if it is ever useful, however far ahead, the sender cannot be accused of keeping it to themselves – indeed can take some credit for their foresight.
- *The 'copies galore' memo*: which is perhaps useful to someone but circulated widely to remind other people of

the writer's existence or importance (e-mail has given the writers of such missives greater opportunity to waste more of others' time).

- *The 'information is power' memo*: sent to few and saying little, but making it clear there are areas of information that are exclusive to the writer.
- *The 'keep off my patch' memo*: which often begins 'It has come to my attention ...' and means 'Back off'.
- *The 'numeracy demonstration' memo*: blinding with figures, confusing with statistics, overpowering with computer print-out, these provide evidence in profusion, perhaps to ensure that the detail is not read.
- *The 'divide and rule' memo*: these, often with different versions of the same message sent to different people, make conflicting points and are usually designed to upset people and get them upset with each other.
- *The 'won't let it lie' memo*: or rather a series of memos relentlessly pursuing, adding to and embellishing a point, long after everyone has lost interest and with the original purpose now totally unaffected.
- *The 'come to a meeting' memo*: as there are, by common assent in most organisations, far too many meetings with far too many people at them (many only present in the hopes of increasing their profile), there are too many of these too.

Memos may inform, but they may also confuse, wind-up or overstate their case. Look at them long and hard – the political content may be considerable. And consider carefully what you put in writing because others will be analysing yours just as carefully.

Finally, remember that the asides in a memo and the style in which it is written say something too. The writer of the apocryphal memo replying to a long, rambling and dictatorial memo insisting on attendance at a training course on the topic of delegation, no doubt took some pleasure in replying to the effect that they were too busy to attend but they would send their assistant! And why not, perhaps this was a point worth making.

How something arrives may be as important as what it says and how it is expressed. Choosing to fax something, mail it or let it take its time will depend on whether you want an instant reaction or to keep someone sweating a while longer. E-mail is much in vogue, but remember how it can overwhelm with sheer quantity and that it can be erased at the touch of a button after the merest glance. Perhaps some things are better given more (potential) permanence.

A final point: use urgency wisely. Getting a reputation for announcing things – whether crisis or triumph – in a way that cries wolf will do your reputation no good at all. But then nor will sitting on things until a minor hiccup has become a full-blown crisis.

On your feet

There is another method of communication that is important, and is also not everybody's forte. That is the skill of making a formal presentation. Few tasks of communication impress so much beyond their content. Presentations can add anything from punch and power to a feeling of considered expertise and certainty.

Or not.

A message that should enthuse and convince may fail simply because of the way it is put across. Plans, budgets, ideas and careers may all stand or fall on the quality of presentation. If you are going to make progress on the organisational stage, and fight your corner successfully, you have to be able to present; and preferably to present well. You not only need to be able to go through things on your feet effectively, but to be in sufficient command of what you are doing to consciously add a feeling of authority, accuracy, urgency, or whatever the occasion demands.

Many people, presenting only with reluctance amongst a welter of ums and ahs, have been excluded from some project or other purely on the strength of the impression this gives of their overall competence. And vice versa; there are those who engineer presentations because they know they excel at them. Next time a presentational opportunity occurs you might check whether you are using the inherent advantages to maximum effect.

The grapevine

Not all communication around an organisation is formal. Every organisation has a grapevine. This network of communication which passes, and sometimes embellishes, news, tittle-tattle and rumour does not relate to the classic hierarchy. Rather it has links based as much on who gets on with who, and even on who is easily accessible to who (for, despite e-mail, people still like to chat face to face).

The points to remember about the grapevine are:

- do not reject it as a rumour machine
- get connected
- listen, and do so carefully
- contribute information as well as listen
- give what you put in feeling as well as fact.

Of course, care is necessary. Not everything you hear will be true. Things need some interpretation, in part by comparing how a message varies between different people. Being 'plugged in' to the grapevine, as it were, may take some organising. You have to have the right contacts if you are to pick up useful information and to do so early in the game. You also need to recognise that its advantages are two way. If you want to circulate information, the first – and sometimes the quickest – thing to do is to whisper it in the right ear. Doing so may simply disseminate the information, or it may bestow particular feeling to it. If you want to hype something up ahead of a meeting about it, then a few well placed comments can get people expressing interest, even approval, and looking forward to the discussion of it. In contrast, seeding suggestions that something is the wrong course of action may be the first step in a campaign to see it stillborn.

Keys to effective communication

Communication has major impact on your level of political success. Every aspect of it needs to be considered judiciously. Particularly:

- Learn the skills of good communication
- Choose methods to match circumstances and objectives
- Remember out-and-out dishonesty rarely helps
- Stay close: ensure you have the contacts you need
- Be visible: ensure people know who you are and what you do
- Do not overdo broadcasting your success (this is resented)
- Never be so insistent or verbose that you become a bore
- Always keep other people's situation in mind and direct your communication appropriately and, if necessary, individually

Management matters

Managers must perform. Objectives must be met and targets reached. Achieving success is key in allowing you to pursue your more personal intentions from a position of strength. If you are responsible for others, for a team of people or department say, then the potential scale of success is greater than what you might achieve alone. Management can be defined as the art of getting things done through other people. Being successful politically goes hand in hand with being a good manager. The better the team performs, and thus the better the overall results, the stronger the position you are in.

Indeed, though today's section is concerned with the process of management, an early career decision should perhaps be to decide whether you seek a path that involves people management or not. Having people report to you certainly demands management skills, and it also contains inherent risks – you stand or fall, to some extent, by the success of your team rather than by what you do personally. It is certainly possible to succeed, wield considerable influence and receive considerable reward within an organisation as an individual operator, however, having a team of people within your remit does increase the opportunities. Effectively it means you have greater resources and a larger stage on which to play out your intentions and ambitions.

Management does not just happen, and the process entails a good deal more than simply allocating work and letting others get on with it. The key management tasks are:

- recruitment and selection
- planning
- organisation
- development
- motivation
- control.

All are important tasks and all contain both political opportunities and pitfalls. The aspiring office politician:

- recognises that management takes time
- studies what makes for effective management
- uses their team to good effect, rather than keeping them in their place
- continuously fine-tunes their own input and their team's performance to maximise achievement of all their objectives.

Recruitment and selection

Finding the right people is clearly important. And doing so successfully should not be underestimated. Few people, despite what they may like to think, are infallible judges of people and thinking you can 'spot the good applicants as they come through the door' is likely to be a recipe for failure. Appointing the wrong people can do untold damage and, especially given what some would regard as labyrinthine employment legislation, can be very difficult to go back on.

Effective recruitment starts with good analysis. Define the job to be done and ascertain the kind of person – in terms of qualifications, experience and expertise – who can best do it. Then go through the selection process systematically and thoroughly. A clear and enticing advertisement is needed. A thorough application form will help screen out those not worth interviewing. Careful interviewing is then called for. You need to give the process sufficient time, perhaps involve colleagues to give you another view, and remember that people are at their best (often an exaggerated best) at interviews. The final advice is definitive: if in doubt do not appoint – especially someone who is no more than the 'best of the (bad?) bunch'.

The big question here is whether you recruit allies or rivals. Appointing 'yes-men' may seem a safe bet (though it is easy to underestimate people in this respect), but the best route is normally only to appoint people who can do a first class job. Supervising the weak or ineffective is hard work, and hardly likely to get you judged as a go-getter.

Planning

Plan the work and work the plan is a good maxim. Set things up well for other people and the success you help them create makes them more likely to be loyal to you. Important things here include:

- defining jobs clearly
- setting standards, objectives and targets agreed after consultation
- making clear control and appraisal procedures (and making them fair)
- planning with people to make their goals attainable (both in terms of what must be done and of methodology).

The ground rules are important. People like to know what is expected of them. They like a challenge, but they also like to feel what they have to do is possible and they like to work for someone who recognises any problems that may stand in the way and who helps them in overcoming them. Sound planning is the foundation to creating a good rapport with your team. Get this wrong, for example setting ill-judged targets it is not realistically possible to achieve, and you forfeit people's goodwill and turn potential allies into people who will spend every possible moment making your life difficult.

Organisation

This is important in two senses. First, if it is down to you to arrange who does what, then the arrangement of people is something that will directly affect productivity, effectiveness and motivation. Struggling to cope amidst the difficulties of apparent poor organisation is frustrating for anyone. Second, you need to keep yourself and your team organised in a time management sense. If no one can ever get anything done because they are in endless, unproductive meetings or struggling with complex systems and paperwork, then your instigation of either will win you no friends.

It is, in fact, easier to run a tight ship, insisting on disciplines that get things done, than to be a laissez faire manager. Your own ambitions are best served by winning respect and that comes most easily through successful management.

Development

High among a manager's responsibilities is that of developing their people. Ask people what they most want in a manager, and they often put 'someone I learn from' at the top of the list. Development means more, much more, than sending people on the occasional course. It encompasses the whole way manager and staff work together, from initial briefing to on-the-job explanation, mentoring and constructive consultation, from departmental meetings to formal training sessions.

It also reflects the dynamic job environment in which we all work today. Things change. Markets, methods, technology – all create the need for constant reconsideration of how things should be done and the need to acquire new skills or upgrade old ones. Recruiting good people, and then managing them in a way that prompts constant improvement, is appreciated by all and will show in the results.

Again this is a way to impress others on a wide front and ensure that your team become real allies. Development may make people more self-sufficient and more innovative and creative. If you succeed or fail by your ability to generate new ideas, do not try to keep the team out of this. Use them. If they have good ideas you all benefit; and you can take the credit for creating a team that is innovative.

Motivation

Never let anyone tell you that the time motivation takes (and it can take a fair amount) is wasted. It is crucial. There is no magic formula. Motivation consists of consideration and action to minimise anything that will lower morale and maximise well being and job satisfaction. Some factors are major. People like to achieve something, they like to know they are achieving something and they like to have the fact acknowledged. Other functions are minor, but they all add up. For example, recognition of achievement is the most powerful element of motivation. Many things are involved in it, including reward and incentive schemes, yet some of it is so simple – just for the manager to say 'Well done'. Simple it may be, but how many of us have done it often enough during, say, the last month?

Motivation is best undertaken with some real knowledge of the people involved. If you get to know your people, what worries them, what satisfies them and how you can work with them to make them feel greater job satisfaction, then not only may better results follow but there is a personal quid per quo. People will walk through fire for the manager who shows they understand and care. When you need an ally, you will have people whose instinct is to support you.

Control

Managers must manage. You may have to lay down the law on occasions. You may have to see that rules are obeyed and that systems and procedures are complied with – and you may have to come on strong sometimes and pull your weight. If you have a team who regard you well, who like working with you, and who understand that some matters must be complied with without debate (perhaps precisely so that time is kept available to act consultively on more important matters), then necessary control is possible. And exercising it should not destroy the acceptability of the management style you adopt.

So, it is possible to be both a popular manager and a successful manager.

There is an important overlap here between management, indeed general people skills, and communication. It occurs when people get together.

Making meetings work

It has been said that the ideal meeting is two – with one absent, and we all know the feeling of frustration stemming from time spent in interminable and unproductive ones. Yet, as with presentations, much may hang on meetings and, more specifically, much may hang on individual performances at meetings. Not all meetings are useful to you, and sometimes the best action is to avoid them. The temptation to be there in case you miss something can be great. It was the author Jilly Cooper who said 'Meetings are rather like cocktail parties. You don't want to go, but you are cross not to be asked.' When you do attend a meeting you must be sure of making a positive impression.

Making meetings work

- Know why the meeting is being held (ask, if necessary, what the objectives are)
- Study the agenda and read all papers circulated beforehand
- Decide what information you may need with you and check your facts
- Discuss as appropriate with others before the meeting to prepare the ground
- Prepare any case you may want to put over
- Be clear regarding the terms of reference for any input you are asked in advance to make (e.g. how much time will you be allowed to make a report)
- Arrive on time
- Obey the rules (e.g. direct comments through the Chair)
- Pull your weight and do not allow yourself to be shouted down
- Listen (and makes notes as necessary)
- Communicate clearly. Be persuasive (or whatever the circumstances demand)
- Be courteous to others (without groveling)

Remember meetings are complex interactions. There is often plenty of subtext and some present may have their own agendas, either to sabotage the published intention or some part of it, or to highjack the meeting, digressing to their own purpose. You need to keep your wits about you, relate to allies and watch for attacks from others. The battle ground analogy here may be all too apt.

There can be a 'last chance' element to meetings. A decision will be made, for good or ill. You may be in a position to prompt the agreement you want, and often this may need a degree of assertiveness (backed by research, facts and hard evidence if necessary). It has been said that if the Creator had a purpose in giving us a neck, then it was surely in the hope that we would sometimes stick it out. And this may well be necessary.

As may other ploys. The astute politician may attend the meeting with three proposals, two which do not quite meet the brief and are designed to be shot down and one, their favorite, which aims to then become the acceptable compromise. Or you may persuade someone else to put up an idea, aiming to inject a variant of it into the argument if it looks like being vetoed. The possibilities are endless, and many people start by forging alliances and coordinating action with others *before* the meeting starts. Having a cunning plan may not be enough. You must have a cunning way of getting it introduced and accepted.

Of course, a meeting may be yours. If so, then you must chair it effectively. Otherwise you may achieve your purpose, but alienate everyone in sight. Whoever is in the chair may be required to be impartial, more often in an organisational setting they have a specified role, and everyone knows what it is. Efficient chairing is respected and, of itself, may help you enhance your profile.

The rules of good chairing

- Aim to command respect
- Come well prepared
- Be on time
- Start on time
- Sort administrative matters early on
- Start on a constructive note
- Refer to and use the agenda
- Introduce people if necessary
- Set, and keep, the rules
- Control the discussion and keep it on track
- Encourage contributions where necessary
- Ask questions and clarify
- Listen … carefully (and make notes)
- Keep an eye on, and manage, the time

- Summarise regularly
- Defuse any outbursts
- Focus on decisions and action
- Highlight action, timing and deadlines applying after the meeting

In meetings the nuances of communication are always important. There is likely to be a need to be diplomatic, assertive, persuasive, empathic, even downright stubborn – and more – in turn. Sometimes manipulation is an appropriate word. For example, the senior individual who introduces something from the chair with a phrase like 'Now I think this is a great idea, what do you think?' creates a wholly different discussion from one who asks for views without pushing their own up front. The former may be ill-considered, loose phraseology or, indeed, used with cynical purpose.

Whatever kind of meeting you attend or run, they are events presenting both opportunities and pitfalls. Committees and regular meetings (such as a monthly departmental meeting) present special problems as they can so often drift away from any clear objectives, and become the office equivalent of a sort of ritual rain dance. Certainly you should think very carefully before agreeing to become a member of some committees: you may be seen as concerned with something unimportant, when you are trying to appear helpful. And time is a valuable resource, which needs to be concentrated on key tasks.

Always be on your guard and remember just because it says 'Review progress on office relocation', say, this does not mean everyone will be focusing on a constructive and practical approach to the problem.

You will do best at meetings if you watch for evidence of:

- hidden agendas
- personal motivations
- playing for time or delaying tactics
- organised alliances
- smokescreens
- blackmail
- spoiling tactics
- flattery
- exaggeration and unwarranted assumption.

In addition to the kind of approaches listed above, you may have to recognise subtle signals and deal with plain old-fashioned bloody-mindedness. When push comes to shove you must organise to play your part well, and at the same time progress your own objectives and enhance your chosen image. This may mean surviving major attack during a presentation for example, but you need to ensure you still end up where you intend.

Management is a prime example of how something that is an inherent part of your role and work can be inextricably linked with projecting and influencing your political standing. Through the way you work with your team and through specific team aspects of operations, like meetings, you can influence both your image and the outcomes of the activity. Management – like most political activity – needs authority. For most this is not something that is given, it is something we create. The confidence with which you exercise it can play a major part in your success.

Active responses and initiatives

If the analogy of the office environment being like a jungle is apt, then, just like someone trying to survive in the jungle, you have to use every means at your disposal to aid your survival. Just as everything you propose to do must be assessed in terms of the utilisation of time if you are to be truly productive, or the financial implications or the cost-effectiveness, so too the political ramifications. This must be a habit. It must be a *reflex*. Your progress in office life is something like snakes and ladders. Spot and take advantage of an opportunity and you can climb a ladder. Fail, even once, to anticipate a potential hazard and you are sliding down a snake.

The game plan

The need to form long-term intentions and to keep the long-term in mind throughout was mentioned in Monday's section. The thought is worth restating here. The Chinese have a saying that a journey of a thousand miles begins with a single step. It is fair comment. You need, at the same time, to bear in mind where you are aiming to get to and to recognise that each step – provided it is in the right direction – takes you just a little nearer. Small steps forward may be worthwhile in themselves, but they may also be disproportionately significant, putting you in a position from which you can more easily move further on.

Time spent on making sure you avoid any kind of setback is useful too. Success comes, major coups apart, from the detail. You need to look out for:

- what can take you forward;
- how you can prevent setbacks

and recognise that many different factors – and people – may play a part.

It is also important to recognise that nothing can be put on one side as fixed or permanently favourable. The environment in any organisation is inherently dynamic. Changes abound – some predictable, others not. Friends become foes, foes become allies and changing circumstances and practices create new opportunities and change the stage upon which the office war is fought out. A new senior manager can change the culture, a move to a new office can change the way communications work and a change in the market can change everything from the amount of money available to the pace of expansion or diversification.

Successful office politicians:

- have clear, long-term intentions
- anticipate change
- review what might help them constantly
- look, creatively, for opportunities to make circumstances work for them
- seek actively to avoid things that might damage their progress
- leave no stone unturned in seeking advantage.

In this section, therefore, we review a number of factors that can be used to secure and strengthen your position and take you on towards your long-term goals. These are as much by way of example as anything. All are common factors, things most people can utilise in their jobs, but individual jobs will doubtless have their own individual factors about which similar attitudes can be taken. From each may stem opportunities to move forward or retrench and prevent backsliding.

Deadlines

All of us have to get things done on time (certainly the manuscript for this book had to be – and was – delivered by a particular date). You can either aim to do so or not.

Hitting deadlines

It is normally in your interests to deliver on time; more than that, to get a reputation for delivering on time. When you meet deadlines you affect other people – you enable them to get on. Your accuracy thus helps others and that may affect your attitude towards how to proceed.

Always challenge a deadline imposed on you if you think it is unreasonable. It may be better to negotiate a different date than agree one reluctantly, struggle and perhaps fail (when, needless to say, your reluctance will never be remembered). And when you hit the time on the nose it may sometimes be worth making sure people notice.

In setting deadlines for others, consult, obtain agreement and then expect delivery to be fulfilled. Never be vague ('let me have it as soon as possible') and give credit where it is due when things are well done.

Playing for time

The moment can pass; sometimes all too easily. So there are occasions when what is best for you (and even for the organisation) is to wait. If others are pressing you, you need reasons for delay, and these must at least seem constructive. For example, you might delay by:

- invoking some other event and its timing – 'Let's look at it again after Christmas'
- involving more people – 'We shouldn't go ahead without knowing John's opinion'
- demanding more detail – 'Let's look at the detailed costing first'
- referring to a higher authority – 'We must let the Board see this'
- putting something else ahead – 'We can only do this after …'
- stressing its importance – 'It's so important, let's not rush into anything'
- commissioning some research – 'We need objective facts here'.

Failing all else convene a committee to take it forward (this could block it forever), though do not expect this to be seen as constructive.

A way to delay can always be found, a way to meet an agreed deadline must be found; the trick is to decide which it is best to do.

Disasters

The Chinese write the word crisis with two separate characters: the first means chaos, and, interestingly, the second means opportunity. Perhaps every cloud can have a silver lining, certainly this is a good way to think about it.

Not everything in business goes well. Sometimes new products fail, research costs a fortune and casts no useful light on anything, budgets are exceeded, newly appointed staff prove useless and a delivery truck demolishes the Managing Director's car. When such things occur you have various options:

- distance yourself from the whole thing – 'I know nothing about it'
- join the 'inquest' – 'We need to find out why this happened'
- look for lessons – 'We must stop this happening again'
- lay blame – 'Of course, it's marketing's responsibility'
- avoid blame – 'Nothing to do with me'
- seek credit – 'I always said it wouldn't work'
- excuse – 'Well, it was an impossible job in the circumstances'.

Or more besides. But whatever line you take bear in mind the realities of human nature: for example, no one ever scored many gold stars for saying 'I told you so', and you may not be popular if you rub people's noses in something (or insist it is put on the record).

If it is your disaster, then things are different. You cannot afford too many disasters, though few people are *always* right. What is necessary if you are to build up a power base is to have a good strike rate. An individual disaster, at least one that it is possible to recover from, will be viewed in the context of your overall record. If not you may want to suggest that it is.

Be very careful about laying blame with others for something that is manifestly your fault. It may get you off the hook in the short term, but make you enemies for life. Reasons are different from excuses. In a dynamic world, there are often changed circumstances – unforeseeable changes, of course – that mean things may not have worked out. There may even be some good that comes from the situation (perhaps being late on something allows new information to be taken into account that changes things for the future); if so this is worth noting.

Whatever the scale of the disaster, there is a position to be taken up and choices to be made. You may only survive by the skin of your teeth, but just being known as a survivor may be useful in itself.

Secretarial support

There is no doubt that a secretary, or at least a good one, can make most jobs easier. Their efficiency helps their bosses achieve more and their ability to improve productivity allows time to be spent on the political front. It is said that behind every successful boss is a secretary making it possible. Perhaps so, but the picture is actually more complicated than that.

Secretaries can be great ambassadors giving an edge to many communications. Consider the following:

- He said it was important that you attend (even if I had to flatter you into it).
- I know she would value your opinion (and passing it on via me is the only way you will get it to her).
- No, I have no idea where he is (though I do know he doesn't want to talk to you today).

There are a thousand and one ways in which a secretary can handle things differently, perhaps more diplomatically, when direct contact yourself might prove more difficult.

The moral here is simple:

- get yourself secretarial assistance if at all possible
- select a good one
- keep them well informed
- involve them and work with them
- give them responsibility
- give them credit.

In other words make them an ally and use them not only to help you meet your job objectives, but to fight your corner too. Even in small ways they may help you score a few points. For example, you alone are upgraded on a flight you are making with a colleague. It is somehow even more annoying for them to be told 'My secretary knows all the right people at the airline'. Do not forget office politics can produce small victories as well as large ones.

Figures

Being numerate is important in any business. Being more numerate than your colleagues can give you an edge. There are a variety of sensitivities regarding figures that you can use. For example, say 'Performance is up about 10.3%' and your credibility will drop (it might be *about* 10%, but 10.3 speaks of accuracy and the juxtaposition of the word 'about' is incongruous). Similarly, be able to cap a discussion replete with various estimates with precision: 'If you work it out you will see it is 12.6% up' commands respect.

Figures provide a classic form of smokescreen. Lies, damn lies and statistics as the saying has it. You can focus on something, avoid the issue, prolong the investigation, or cut through the uncertainties given the right number. Make certain you are sure of your facts, then the choice is yours and the range of possible outcomes is considerable.

And of course, all the above comment is doubly true of figures of a financial nature. Money talks. You need to make it say what you want.

Attending a course

Training is a good thing: that would certainly be the attitude in many organisations. This is not just a motherhood statement; the dynamic nature of the modern business world demands training is taken seriously. People have to develop; even the best performance can be improved and old skills need updating and new ones adding to everyone's portfolio.

Two factors should be born in mind:

- Being seen to be in favour of training (for yourself and any staff you have) is the best attitude to adopt; the image is positive, more so if you manifestly practice what you preach and use training.
- You will likely need training and development over time; do not put this off, rather put yourself in the position to benefit from any training done as soon as possible.

That said other details matter too:

Identify training needs
Have a rolling plan for development. What is it worth or necessary spending time on? Update your view of this constantly, document it and get approval (and budget) for it if necessary.

Select the method
Think about the best way to meet any development need. This may range widely, from reading a book to taking six months at a business school in the States. You may need to choose between one-off inputs (such as short courses), and something longer term (including distance learning) with a qualification awarded following any success. And if a provider is to be involved, think about both the practicalities involved and the kudos. More than one manager has been known to keep the car park entry ticket to a prestigious management college on their car long after the course has finished, others simply keep quiet about their trips to somewhere low key.

Maximise the benefit
Take training seriously. On courses, pay attention, take notes, prepare and ask questions, and try to relate content and coverage to the real world of work. Consider also the people aspects of the event: note who is there, discover whether they can help you in future, forge any useful alliances, and keep in touch as appropriate after the programme has finished.

Follow through
Think about who needs to know you have been involved in training. Consider: would a debriefing session with your line manager be useful, with the organisation's training manager or your staff? And what action can you take

following training – new ways of doing things, experiments to try, further training to arrange? Returning to a desk piled high after an absence makes it easy to put things off. Prompt action may be the only way to get the best from such opportunities.

Not finding time for development, or going about it in an unplanned ad hoc way, is highly likely to reduce your chances of success.

Records

Your ability to act, and where necessary act quickly, is strongly linked to your store of information. Information is power, yet a compromise is always involved here. You could spend your life doing nothing but filing and create a situation in which you cannot squeeze into your own office because of the stacks of papers. Or you can throw everything away regardless. Somewhere between these extremes you will have to find a happy medium.

It is the usefulness of information that counts. You do not need to file a memo summoning you to an important meeting, whereas you may well need to be able to find the minutes without difficulty (too much in files can make finding the important things more difficult).

Consider every item you might salt away:

- should you file it?
- where?
- for how long?
- under what heading?

Files need organising, cleaning (for example filing things linked to a destroy date) and records need updating. It is worth the effort, but the task must be systematised and minimised. Quite apart from its usefulness to you, being able to produce something someone else needs instantly and unfailingly is impressive (or annoying, and both may be useful).

Contracts and agreements

One thing that does need filing is anything that is of a binding nature. Negotiating the details of a deal is important, so negotiation is another career skill for the office politician. Once things are agreed and in writing then change may become much more difficult. So, when binding agreements are in the offing – whether in the form of a job description or a business arrangement for which you have responsibility – always:

- think before you act
- aim high
- negotiate hard
- trade variables rather than concede points
- aim for both parties to feel it is a good deal (the win-win scenario of negotiation).

Remember that, after agreement has been made, it becomes a basis for operation (at least for a while). You must be able to live with it, and recognise that reneging on an agreement can undermine your carefully cultivated profile in a big way.

Work and success

What you do and how well you do it both have a direct impact on how you are perceived. Core responsibilities are one thing, but many jobs are, to some extent at least, a series of projects. Again there are choices to be made. Projects vary in their profile. You may want to take on challenging things, knowing that if you succeed the word will go round (be sent round, perhaps) and your image will receive a boost. You may want to avoid things too. Make 300 people redundant, close down one of the factories or delete something from the product range and you may be seen as a butcher ... or a tough operator prepared to tackle difficult matters head on.

Some projects are almost guaranteed to cause you grief. Some things, perhaps ones as seemingly simple as organising an event to celebrate the firm's 25th anniversary, are never going to please everyone and you may resist being the one to alienate one group, especially over something where feelings run high.

Extra-curricular activity

Another area where the pros and cons have to be weighed up carefully, and where not just the usefulness of something but how it makes you seem is important, concerns activities that overflow outside the organisation.

There are a host of activities of this nature in which you might consider getting involved, for example:

- sitting on (or chairing) an external committee (at a trade organisation perhaps)
- participating in a professional body (a branch of the Institute of Management, say)
- speaking at a conference
- undertaking a public relations role for the organisation (anything from writing an article to being interviewed on local radio)
- liaising with an outside body (something regulatory, perhaps).

Sex

The hazards of sex in the office are not the issue here (though there are those who should think about the appropriateness of their liaisons). Perhaps the better word is gender. Women are, for the most part, not the junior partners in organisations that they often were years ago. Of course there is still prejudice, though it is not impossible that women direct it at men as much as the other way round. Both sexes need to tread warily. Without getting into the obvious pitfalls of sexual harassment, dealing with members of the opposite sex needs additional considerations over and above other interaction.

Let us be clear here. Do not be misled; it is possible that someone may be a competitor, opponent or simply more interested in their own situation than yours – regardless of sex. It is important:

- not to typecast people
- not to display prejudice, even unintentionally
- not to appear resentful
- not to underestimate anyone's capabilities or power
- not to allow yourself to appear 'the inferior woman/man'.

Small things do need watching. It is possible, for example, that the sole woman at a meeting electing, helpfully or just thirstily, to pour the coffee sends out the wrong signals. If this is so, you may want to change attitudes. This takes time, so the immediate task is to avoid such perceptions – whichever way round they occur.

Of course, there are times when being a man or woman, or dealing with one or the other, makes a difference to the way things must be handled, but – for the most part – the best tactic is dealing with any differences without labouring the point.

Summary

The examples in this section make a clear point. Some things form a useful part of your profile. Others magnify the good effect by being excluded. But the impact also depends on how such things go: a good radio interview might have people talking about you in awed terms for weeks to come. A bad one might make you an instant laughing stock.

With all the topics dealt with in this chapter, and more, the lesson is the same. Everything must be considered in terms of how it may affect your standing, everything must be examined to see if it presents an opportunity, or if it is a sign of hidden danger to come. Careful reaction, in the light of your short-term and long-term intentions, can enhance your situation.

Beyond that, you need to constantly monitor your progress, asking whether your current position demands defensive action or allows further progress to be made. It is to this that we turn for the final day's review.

Consolidating your position

If you are aware of the need to take office politics into account, indeed to do something about it, then consolidation is very much the first step to being able to survive – and thrive. In addition, as the previous chapters have made clear, there are skills involved and there is a need for constant vigilance and fine-tuning as you move ahead – ideally with a clear plan of what you want to achieve.

Success does not mean you can relax. There is always the possibility of setback or reversal, and you need to act to consolidate and maintain your position. As has been said, success comes not from some magic formula, but from the details. However, to keep things manageable we will concentrate here on four additional factors before summarising the overall picture.

Constant monitoring

The need for constant awareness cannot be overstated. You need to keep an eye on everything and everybody, recognising that things can change very quickly if you take your eye off the ball. All sorts of things distract, for example:

- pressure of work
- tackling new things
- feeling all is well
- being reassured by others that all is well
- focusing on one issue, to the exclusion of others.

Despite the distraction and the pressure, you need to monitor your political standing and progress constantly. In passing, it should perhaps be noted that those who are most successful in an organisation are rarely those that are most stressed out. Stress is, after all, a reaction to pressure. By managing the pressure, and by remaining essentially laid back about things, you are more likely to remain in control and on top of the situation. You should constantly monitor:

- your plan and intentions
- your progress and career development
- the opportunities and pitfalls in your work environment
- the people around you and how they might help or hinder you.

The intention should always be to have a view of how to handle matters next. Is there a difficulty you foresee that will need overcoming? Is there an opportunity that lends itself to some ploy? Or do you simply need to heighten your profile or build it up positively in some specific way?

Confidence

A quotation encapsulates an important thought: 'If you think you can, you can. And if you think you can't, you're right' (Mary Kay Ash). You need to have the courage of your convictions and confidence in your ability to succeed. If you want to take on a particular project, say, then it helps if you truly believe that you can complete it successfully – and even that you can do it better than anyone else. If you can think like this it helps. If not, ask what would make such feelings possible. If you can only take something on after some advice, training or rehearsal, so be it. Get down to organising the preliminaries and then go for it with confidence.

Two results of confidence

- Believing you can succeed helps you do so.
- Appearing confident makes it more likely that others will believe you can succeed.

Put yourself in a position where you are able to be confident and you make success more likely.

Working the system

Being politically successful does not necessarily need constant contrivance. Most of the opportunities you need are all around you, they are an inherent part of the ongoing life and processes of the organisation for which you work. All that is necessary is to recognise the possibilities that are there, and take advantage of them. Opportunities are inherent in:

- meetings
- projects
- processes
- systems
- changes
- information
- people.

So, whatever the circumstances – you have an appraisal scheduled, you are recruiting a new member of staff, you are giving a presentation to the Board, or writing a report that will be widely circulated – you not only need to have the possibilities stemming from it in mind, you need to make them work.

It is the way you orchestrate the possibilities that is perhaps most important. An anecdote may serve as a good example at this point. I once met someone in the studios of LBC (the London talk radio station). He was being interviewed on some technical matter to do with industry – chemical engineering, I think. I asked if he headed the technical department, and will always remember his answer. He said 'No, but I will.' Not only did he lack nothing in confidence, but that was his plan. Taking advantage of an opportunity to be on radio (which he had helped engineer and executed very well) played to his strengths and created visibility in a way that he knew would raise his image. Becoming the company spokesperson on his subject was likely to be an effective part of his game plan. But the interview needed doing and doing well. Numbers of people might have done it – but he had staked a claim and was determined not only to do a good job, but also to gain from it. This is exactly the kind of creative orchestration of skills and circumstances that often works best.

A degree of ruthlessness

While we might prefer that honest dealing was all that corporate success required, we know this is sometimes not the case. Like so much else there is a balance needed. Out-and-out ruthlessness and dishonesty may be self-defeating, especially when brute force is applied unthinkingly. We all tend to applaud when the bully gets their come-uppance (although some succeed for longer than we would like).

On the other hand, it would be dishonest to suggest that there are never occasions for some element of ruthlessness. You must judge carefully how far you take matters. Certainly success is based to some degree on all the following. Sometimes, and to some extent, you need to be:

- assertive
- strong willed
- stubborn
- firm
- resolute in the long term
- persuasive
- forceful.

Skills are involved here and there may be abilities you need to cultivate to strengthen your overall chances of operating successfully. Certainly you need to be prepared to stick to your guns and fight your corner where necessary. Much can be achieved through diplomacy (another useful skill); some things need a more head-on approach. And sometimes action that others at least will see as devious is the only route forward. The tougher you propose to be, the more perhaps you need to think through the consequences.

You need the ability to be diplomatic or forceful – and to select which is best in which individual circumstances.

Having added the comments above to extend the overall picture, we will now pull things together and summarise the essentials.

The week in summary

Over the week, we have covered a variety of aspects of office life and, whatever else, it will be clear that there is no magic formula for winning out politically. You must work at it, and you must do so consciously and with due consideration of all the changing people and circumstances surrounding you. No stone must be left unturned and if you take your eye off the ball, you may find you have missed something significant.

The positive and negative sides of the process are equally important. It can be as useful to spot and take advantage of an opportunity as to sidestep a problem. Or identify an adversary sufficiently clearly and far ahead so that you can take preventative action to neutralise their impact on your progress.

Three areas are touched on here in conclusion.

1. Planning pays dividends

There is no doubt that you will normally do better if you approach the political process with clear intentions. Your career needs active planning anyway. No one can rely on a 'job for life' these days; no one should rely on good luck to see them through (though, of course, you *can* explain *others'* success exclusively on the basis of good luck!).

Charting a course through the choppy, politically uncertain waters of the corporate environment is only an element of active career development. You need to be clear what you want to do, and work to secure your chosen outcome despite the distractions and hazards appearing in – or placed in – your way.

Be clear in your intentions and work to achieve them.

2. Flexibility enhances your success

A plan is useful, though you must not allow your intentions to become fixations and take over your life. But prediction is an inexact science. You will never anticipate all the things that may crop up along the way to help or hinder you. But you can aim to anticipate as many as possible, and to react positively to everything – making decisions and taking actions that fine-tune your progress and maximise your chances of success.

Aim to be 'quick on your feet', keeping your wits about you and adapting your action in light of the actual circumstances.

3. Survive and prosper

At the end of the day it is down to you. Remember what Lily Tomlin said: 'We're all in this together. By ourselves.' In fact no one is without help, we all forge alliances and, although they may change over time, they are always part of how we operate. But it is your talents for the process that will help you most.

The following is not intended to be a definitive list, but all those characteristics listed are important and those chosen illustrate the diversity of approaches and skills that are demanded. If you are to survive and perhaps turn organisational politicking to your own good you must have:

- *Knowledge of what is going on* – which means good sources and lines of information
- *The right people on your side* – whether influencers, sources of information or close allies and whether voluntarily, unknowingly, or because they have their arm twisted
- *Good communications skills* – verbal, written, formal and informal
- *The 'right' image* – an accurate idea of what is suitable and the right degree of visibility
- *The patience of a saint* – and certainly the ability to see the broad picture, implement a long-term strategy and, if necessary, bide your time
- *Sufficient assertiveness* – this balances the patience; it is important to be prepared to fight your corner and to be seen to have sufficient clout to do so (though being aggressive may not help)

- *Organisational and management abilities* – there will be no time to consider political matters, much less do anything about them, if time, people, projects and yourself are not well managed
- *Fleetness of foot* – you need to spot potential pitfalls and opportunities, have an eye for the main chance and the wit to take advantage of it
- *A degree of ruthlessness* – not least with yourself, and the sensitivity to know when not to overdo it with others so that it becomes self-defeating.

So, if you cultivate and deploy such characteristics all will go well, and you will stay on top of things. If so, then there will be some moments when the pressure will ease and you can relax a little, confident that you are safely on course. But, realistically, there is never a moment when you can be off your guard. Honestly, trust me (and trust your instincts next time someone in your office says something like this to you – and read between the lines!).

Nothing new

As a post script it might be borne in mind that all this is nothing new. Modern organisational life certainly adds some new wrinkles, and the pace of change means that the detail of the way office politics works may sometimes change as you watch, but essentially the battle is something that has gone on for as long as people have interacted and will doubtless continue to do so. This is evidenced by such comments as:

"Politics is not a science ... but an art"
Bismarck (1884)

"Man is by nature a political animal".
Aristotle (said some 300 years BC)

"Politics is a blood sport".
Aneurin Bevan

All of the above make as much sense in an organisation as they do in the governmental sense of politics. Also apt, and more recent, is another quotation:

"A politician is an animal that can sit on a fence and keep two ears to the ground".
H.L. Menkin

Your having to cope with office politics is not a plot, it is not personal, it is just one of the givens of organisational life. The only response is an active approach that aims to put you at an advantage.

Further *Successful Business in a Week* titles from Hodder & Stoughton and the Institute of Management all at £6.99

0 340 71205 8	Appraisals in a Week	❒
0 340 70546 9	Assertiveness in a Week	❒
0 340 71197 3	Benchmarking in a Week	❒
0 340 57640 5	Budgeting in a Week	❒
0 340 74751 X	Bullying at Work in a Week	❒
0 340 72077 8	Business Growth in a Week	❒
0 340 70540 X	Business on the Internet in a Week	❒
0 340 71199 X	Business Plans in a Week	❒
0 340 62103 6	Business Process Re-engineering in a Week	❒
0 340 59813 1	Business Writing in a Week	❒
0 340 71200 7	Communication at Work in a Week	❒
0 340 62032 3	Computing for Business in a Week	❒
0 340 73781 6	Consultancy in a Week	❒
0 340 74752 8	Credit Control in a Week	❒
0 340 71196 5	Customer Care in a Week	❒
0 340 70543 4	CVs in a Week	❒
0 340 72076 X	Dealing with Difficult People in a Week	❒
0 340 63154 6	Decision Making in a Week	❒
0 340 73762 X	Delegation in a Week	❒
0 340 62741 7	Direct Mail in a Week	❒
0 340 73048 X	E-mail in a Week	❒
0 340 64330 7	Empowerment in a Week	❒
0 340 66374 X	Environmental Management in a Week	❒
0 340 71192 2	Finance for Non-Financial Managers in a Week	❒
0 340 71189 2	Flexible Working in a Week	❒
0 340 67925 5	Fundraising and Sponsorship in a Week	❒
0 340 71204 X	Going Freelance in a Week	❒
0 340 65487 2	Human Resource Management in a Week	❒
0 340 74287 9	Information Overload in a Week	❒
0 340 74756 0	Interviewing in a Week	❒
0 340 71179 5	Intranets in a Week	❒
0 340 63152 X	Introducing Management in a Week	❒
0 340 71203 i	Introduction to Bookkeeping and Accounting in a Week	❒
0 340 71202 3	Leadership in a Week	❒
0 340 71173 6	Management Gurus in a Week	❒
0 340 65503 8	Managing Change in a Week	❒
0 340 63153 8	Managing Information in a Week	❒
0 340 74757 9	Marketing in a Week	❒
0 340 47579 7	Marketing Plans in a Week	❒
0 340 57466 6	Market Research in a Week	❒
0 340 60894 3	Meetings in a Week	❒
0 340 74241 0	Memory Techniques in a Week	❒
0 340 61137 5	Mentoring in a Week	❒
0 340 71174 4	Mind Maps® in a Week	❒
0 340 73761 1	Motivation in a Week	❒
0 340 70545 0	Negotiating in a Week	❒
0 340 64341 2	Networking in a Week	❒
0 340 71123 X	Neuro-Linguistic Programming in a Week	❒
0 340 73812 X	Office Feng Shui in a Week	❒
0 340 72073 5	Personal Investment in a Week	❒
0 340 70541 8	Planning Your Own Career in a Week	❒
0 340 70544 2	Presentation in a Week	❒
0 340 71208 2	Process Management in a Week	❒
0 340 70539 6	Project Management in a Week	❒
0 340 64761 2	Problem Solving in a Week	❒
0 340 73780 8	Psychometric Testing in a Week	❒
0 340 56479 2	Public Relations in a Week	❒
0 340 71206 6	Purchasing in a Week	❒
0 340 61888 4	Quality Management Standards in a Week	❒
0 340 73816 2	Recruitment in a Week	❒
0 340 71198 1	Report Writing in a Week	❒
0 340 70538 8	Selling in a Week	❒
0 340 67397 4	Selling on the Internet in a Week	❒
0 340 65504 6	Statistics in a Week	❒
0 340 72494 3	Strategy in a Week	❒
0 340 71201 5	Stress Management in a Week	❒
0 340 70542 6	Succeeding at Interviews in a Week	❒
0 340 71207 4	Teambuilding in a Week	❒
0 340 70547 7	Time Management in a Week	❒
0 340 71191 4	Total Quality Management in a Week	❒
0 340 71195 7	Training in a Week	❒
0 340 62102 8	VAT in a Week	❒
0 340 67905 0	Virtual Organisation in a Week	❒
0 340 70508 6	Web Sites in a Week	❒

All Hodder & Stoughton books are available from your local bookshop or can be ordered direct from the publisher. Just tick the titles you want and fill in the form below. Prices and availability subject to change without notice.

To: Hodder & Stoughton Ltd, Cash Sales Department, Bookpoint, 39 Milton Park, Abingdon, Oxon, OX14 4TD. If you have a credit card you may order by telephone – 01235 400414.

E-mail address: orders@bookpoint.co.uk

Please enclose a cheque or postal order made payable to Bookpoint Ltd to the value of the cover price and allow the following for postage and packaging:

UK & BFPO: £4.30 for one book; £6.30 for two books; £8.30 for three books.

OVERSEAS & EIRE: £4.80 for one book; £7.10 for 2 or 3 books (surface mail).

Name: ....

Address: ....

....

If you would prefer to pay by credit card, please complete:

Please debit my Visa/Mastercard/Diner's Card/American Express (delete as appropriate) card no:

❒ ❒ ❒ ❒ ❒ ❒ ❒ ❒ ❒ ❒ ❒ ❒ ❒ ❒ ❒ ❒

Signature .... Expiry Date ....